HOW TO PRAY ALWAYS

How to Pray Always

Principles and Practices for Attaining
to Union with God

By Raoul Plus, S.J.

Translated by Irene Hernaman

THE NEWMAN PRESS
WESTMINSTER, MARYLAND
1948

NIHIL OBSTAT:

EDWARDUS MAHONEY, S.T.D..
Censor deputatus.

IMPRIMATUR:

EDM. CAN. SURMONT,
Vicarius generalis.

WESTMONASTERII,
Die 29ª Martii, 1926.

INTRODUCTION

GOD is dwelling in us. Everyone in a state of grace bears the most high God in him, in the Real Presence.

This is a fact, a reality, a certainty.

Some people when confronted by this fact, either for the first time or after long consideration, may be tempted, and many are tempted, to say to themselves: "Since God condescends to dwell habitually with me, my one wish is to dwell continually with him. My aim from henceforward will be never to lose the recollection of his presence for a single moment. Our Lord himself taught us to pray without ceasing;[1] my life shall become an incessant prayer, and I shall begin this very day."

Now how far is it possible to put this ideal into practice, and how much is really attainable; how can the implications of this injunction, to pray without ceasing, be reconciled with the requirements of our psychological self and our daily life; how can we reach a right understanding of the conflicting call of the invisible world within us and the imperious and quite legitimate demands of the visible world without, and reconcile the attractions of a life that we should like to be as contemplative as possible with the duties of an active life—in a few words, how is it possible

[1] 1 Thess. v 17.

to reach a correct understanding of the meaning of recollection and the correct balance between generosity and wisdom? It is these points which will be explained in these pages.

Three fundamental principles govern these considerations:

1. A principle of psychology: it is impossible (exceptional cases apart) to fix our minds always upon God.

2. A moral principle: to be one with God in will is better than continual recollection.

3. A principle of ascetic theology: the frequent thought of God is of great assistance in reaching the intimate union of the will with God.

These ideas may be expressed more briefly without interfering with subsequent fuller explanations, by saying:

To think always of God is impossible.

To be thinking always of God is not necessary.

It is most profitable to think often of God.

These three principles having been laid down, it remains to be seen how the practice of a life of perfect recollection is governed by three laws:

To pray well.

To turn everything into prayer.

To spread abroad the spirit of prayer.

CONTENTS

vii

CONTENTS

PART II

THE PRACTICAL SIDE

PART I
THE PRINCIPLES

CHAPTER I

TO THINK ALWAYS OF GOD IS IMPOSSIBLE

1. *Why this is impossible.*
2. *Our present difficulty in thinking continuously of God for any length of time.*

I

THERE is a distinction to be made at the outset, which will throw a strong light upon this problem. We must be on our guard to avoid confusing the *act* of prayer with the *state* of prayer.

Further on we shall see in what consists the state of prayer.

An act of prayer may be either vocal or mental, according as it is formed of words recited by the lips, or is the inner cry of the soul expressed in formulated or unformulated transports of love, or in the silence of union with God. In these two cases our thoughts are occupied or trying to be occupied with God.

Our acts of prayer are the moments when our thoughts are in loving union with God.

The problem is this : can these moments of loving union with our Lord be brought so close together that they form one almost continuous chain of thought ? More briefly : can my thoughts be absorbed without intermission with God; is it possible to think of nothing but him?

No. Here lies a double impediment; first the practical impossibility. Our daily duties involve a number of actions other than formulated acts of prayer. There may be a lesson to prepare, a lecture to give, some household task or work of charity to be attended to, or an engrossing intellectual study to be undertaken. And if it is true that it is very difficult to think of one thing while doing another, in most cases and for most people an occupation, even when only external, absorbs all their energies, including those of the mind. This is due to our natural frailty. Later we shall endeavour to show how a wise method can somewhat get over this obstacle, but the fact remains. Hemmed in as we are by the visible world of sense, it is only with difficulty that we can have even fragmentary relations with the invisible world. Man is created with a body and soul, and no one can ask of others or require of himself to lead a life of pure spirit.

To this practical difficulty is added another of a psychological character. Even if our occupations were reduced to the minimum, and if, as is the case with a contemplative vocation, we were able to spend a large portion of time in prayer, yet continuous prayers would be impossible, for they would soon lead to grave mental derangement and complete powerlessness.

4

We are not archangels. Even the time-table of the contemplative orders is interspersed with other occupations than contemplative prayer. No one can be continually adding fresh prayers to his usual exercises. It is, then, an illusion to wish never to lose the recollection of God for one instant. Our mental powers are incapable of this.

Doubtless God can endow the soul with special faculties, so as to enable her to live always or nearly always with the thought or consciousness of his presence. In such a case, the ability to remain in the presence of God is not the normal result of our own efforts. It is the action of God, who delights in overwhelming the soul. He enfolds it in a recollection that is more or less impenetrable to outside disturbances. Mystical writers call this infused recollection, to distinguish it from that which is the result of our own efforts and is called acquired recollection. This recollection can progress from the simple mystic touch, which is temporary and often of very short duration, to a union that is continuous. In this case, recollection is permanent, suffering no eclipse of the beloved presence and its enjoyment.

At first this may lead to moments of such entire absorption that the soul is more or less unfitted to take its place in its accustomed surroundings: that which is seen within is so different from the painted canvas of the outside world. But in the highest stage of union the

5

soul finds it can easily adjust its sense life to harmonize with its supernatural life : outwardly it behaves like everyone else, while keeping within perpetual contact with the divine Master. It is bound and it is free, and all the freer for being bound to him who is sovereign liberty, on whom it is entirely dependent.

The masters of the spiritual life are unanimous in recognizing that persons who are favoured with this highest degree of union with God are rare. They are less in agreement over the question as to whether there are few or many who are endowed with periods of infused recollection. They are unanimous in reckoning that in all probability this infused power of recollection is unattainable by human means, and that none can claim it as a right, however great their efforts may have been. It is the opinion of some writers that if someone who is mentally adaptable and subject to no hindrances gives himself up to leading a prayerful and mortified life in as perfect a degree as possible, he will in fact reach the state of infused recollection, although it is in no sense his due. They declare that God is so desirous of giving himself that whenever he finds one who is well disposed and detached, he will most certainly communicate himself. Others question this statement. It is true that man was created for the vision of God, but that will be granted to him at the end of his earthly existence.

6

We walk by faith as wayfarers in this world. To say that every mortified soul is called upon to quit this life of faith and enter now into direct possession, is to turn these persons into merely semi-wayfarers. Another objection is that there are persons who have practised detachment during the course of a long life, yet in spite of apparently being quite suitable, they have never experienced even the shadow of a mystical favour.

This is not the place in which to take part in a discussion of this sort. In every case infused recollection, whether it be the normal outcome of acquired recollection or not, is in itself and by right independent of our own efforts, so that it is impossible to lay down technical rules concerning it, and still less to give any infallible advice as to how to prepare for it.

II

Acquired recollection is quite another thing. It depends entirely upon ourselves, aided of course by the grace of God, but grace of a usual character.

All the same it is necessary to define the extent and limitations of the power of man over his imagination, senses, and thoughts. Man has direct control over his thoughts. I can think about what I like. But our authority over the imagination and senses is different. Here we have only indirect control. Mental pictures and reactions find their way

7

in and work away within us without our
assistance ; indeed, often they are against us.
All we can do is to place ourselves in a
favourable environment amid peaceful conditions. But I cannot prevent that idea from
crossing my brain. I may try to forbid
the entrance of certain ideas into my mind,
yet they will come in all the same, but at
any rate I shall not have given them any
assistance. The imagination and feeling are
a couple of giddy-pates. I may circumscribe
their field of action, but to keep them entirely
within bounds is impossible. At the very
moment when I am most anxious to be at
peace, when saying my prayers or during
some engrossing work, they worm their way
in, and sometimes take complete possession of
my thoughts.

The conclusion to be drawn from these
psychological truths is that the possibility of
success in recollection is both very great and
very small.

The possibility is small because our memory
and imagination are incessantly trying to
distract our attention in spite of us, and
sometimes God only knows how they manage
to do it. St Jerome in the desert was tor-
mented by the thought of Roman festivities ;
St Antony by fantastic visions which are
depicted for us in sacred art. The possibility
is great, for have we not the power at each
moment of forcibly recalling some incident or

idea to our mind ; and, above all, are we not our own masters, and able to drive away the proximate causes of distraction?

Every spiritual writer insists upon this point when speaking of the remote preparation for prayer.

If we madly throw ourselves into worldly frivolous amusements and pleasures, even though they are quite harmless, we have no right to complain of remaining for long moments without thinking of God, and of spiritual dryness and dullness at prayer.

" I really tried to pray," we say, " and I can do nothing. It is quite sufficient for me to kneel down at my prie-dieu for distractions to come tumbling into my mind immediately, like sparrows fluttering down to pick up crumbs, and for them to torment me without a second's respite."

But what about the crumbs you collected when you left your mind open to every form of distraction, idle conversations, frivolous books, inquisitiveness? Naturally, once you were still your imagination had full play with all these thoughts.

There is an art in keeping a watch over our thoughts, in clearing the brain, sifting our impressions, and in getting rid of idle fancies. If every trivial thought can enter the mind as if it were a mill, and cast any rubbish it likes under the grindstone, whose fault is it that later on, instead of the homogeneous white flour of pure wheat, there is only worthless chaff? As nothing can be really destroyed unless something else takes its place, so the difficulty is less how to drive away useless impressions and ideas from the mind and the imagination, than to suggest some profitable thoughts to these two faculties; we ought to endeavour to live habitually with a number of holy impressions and ideas stored up in our minds.

Hence we discover a curiously vicious circle.

The best means of preserving habitual recollection is fidelity to prayer.

The best condition for praying well is habitual recollection. It is not without reason that St Ignatius recommends the man who wishes to pray well to prepare the subject of his prayer on the preceding evening, so as to occupy the memory. Then he goes to rest with these thoughts in his mind; on waking he will call to mind the subject-matter of his meditation prepared the evening before, and think quietly about it while dressing. This is the advice of one who was a master of asceticism and also an expert in psychology.

When the moment for prayer arrives, he recommends that if the person is alone he shall not immediately kneel down, but remain standing some distance away and reflect upon the presence of God there in that room, then kiss the ground as an act of humiliation and so associate the body with the religious attitude of the mind.

This is the *immediate preparation* which completes the remote preparation. It is easy to call these mere details; anyone who has really tried to meditate will readily allow that this is sensible advice. The Church has the same end in view when she tells us on entering the church to take holy water and make the sign of the cross. Her aim is to impress upon the mind of the incomer the idea of the proximity of God. It is a great mistake to try and pray as some people do, immediately after leaving some absorbing work, without any interval, and then expect, as soon as they are on their knees, the mind to be at rest and divine thoughts to come flowing in. Man is one complete whole: there are no water-tight compartments in him. Our whole self enters into every movement of our activity. It requires extraordinary agility of mind to be able to leave behind on the other side of the door everything that would be a hindrance to our devotions. Sometimes, in spite of our good intentions and determined efforts, it is impossible to control our thoughts during prayer. How much more likely is this to occur if the will has not foreseen and guarded against the approach of danger.

The practice of prayer, also, is the best preparation for a recollected life.

It is necessary to introduce into the mind a number of ideas and impressions which will be of use in prayer. Nothing will be of greater assistance than the fixed determination to come into daily close contact with God. To quote the words of the foundress of the Oblates of the Sacred Heart, Louise de Montaignac: "It is by accustoming ourselves to making acts of love at regular moments that we shall learn the good habit of being able to turn to God at all times."

It is a foolish mistake to expect to lead a recollected life that is not also a life of prayer. The best method of learning to pray always, is to pray whenever it is possible, and as well as is possible.

CHAPTER II

TO BE THINKING ALWAYS OF GOD IS NOT NECESSARY

1. *The state of prayer and our daily duties.*
2. *Our Lord, the model of the state of prayer.*

I

FATHER QUADRAPANI the Barnabite tells us in one of his books that "To do all our actions for God is worth more than thinking about him."

This statement, if rightly understood, is quite correct. But it has nothing to do with deciding whether the active or the contemplative life is the more perfect state. This question was settled long ago, and is quite outside the present considerations. It matters not whether a life be contemplative or not, in the cloister or in the world—the point is this: what is it that God asks of us, apart from the times of stated prayer? Is it to think about him, or rather and above all to do our actions for him? Is it our mind that he wants, or our heart, our memory, or our will? Unquestionably it is our will. With the exception of the time of prayer, when our acts for God consist in thinking of him, God demands that on every occasion we should be working for him, even, if necessary, by restraining the thought of him when—and the supposition is not fanciful—it would be to the detriment of our work for him.

A concrete example will make this clear.

A mother of a family finds herself over-burdened with urgent household tasks: there are the children who are still young; her reduced staff of servants, which obliges her to attend to the management of the house herself; because she is ill instructed in her duties, the morning finds her going off to Mass and absorbed in long and maybe fervent prayers when prudence demands that she should stay at home and see to the care of the house.

Is she following the exact path that God has traced out for her, or that an enlightened piety would require?

Or let us suppose that the morning Mass is possible, but that the mother on her return to her family is so absorbed by her pious thoughts that she does nothing well. The moments of prayer increase, her ejaculations and aspirations accumulate, but so do the garments to be mended, and all sorts of things are forgotten and left undone. Who is there who would not advise, in a case like this, fewer pious exercises and greater fidelity to home duties?

It is quite clear that whenever duty requires us to pray, then all our efforts should be exerted in trying to think about God as fully as is possible.

14

Apart from this, where does our duty lie? It demands that the act of the present moment shall be done *for* God as perfectly as possible, that in all that I do I shall not look for self-satisfaction, but that God alone shall be my final objective. This last sentence expresses in brief the whole theory of how "*to pray always.*"

To be always praying does not imply a succession of religious exercises one after the other—five decades of the rosary followed by a little office, then a spiritual reading, with mental prayer to come after it, and so on—but to live in *a state* in which everything is the means whereby "the soul is lifted up to God." No one can attempt to turn his life into an uninterrupted succession of pious exercises, or the mental balance will be rapidly upset.

Our aim should be to guard against the danger of worldliness by acting always with a pure intention, so that our whole life may be offered up to God.

Continuous *acts* of prayer are *impossible;* the continuous *state* of prayer is highly desirable.

The state of prayer consists in preserving a pure intention during the fulfilment of our daily tasks. I cannot have my thoughts occupied with God without interruption. But my will should never be directed towards any object except God, at any rate as its last end.

15

To refer all that we do implicitly, though not always explicitly, to God through this direct orientation of the will, is a form of union with him that is both quite attainable and leads to perfection.

The difficulty then resolves itself into this: how to keep the *will* in this fixed direction towards God in all our actions. It is the whole problem of the *direction of the intention*. There are many ways of directing the intention towards God: by thinking of him at the present moment—*actual* intention; or, without thinking of him at this moment, by acting under the impulse of an intention formulated earlier, which still persists—a *virtual* intention.

Some people are inclined to think that an *habitual* good intention is sufficient to render our acts supernaturally meritorious. They declare that from the fact that there has been no positive deviation from the path that the soul has mapped out, therefore it continues along the straight course towards God, and eternal merit is retained.

According to this hypothesis, every human act that is not bad tends towards God, and is therefore an act that can be supernatural-ized and lifted up to God; it is at the same time a prayer and a meritorious act.

If we apply this statement to the virtual intention, all is well. In a fervent soul the whole activity is governed by clearly defined

16

supernatural motives, so that the virtual intention is nearly always present.

Therefore, in the life of a truly generous and Christlike soul, if we distinguish between prayers taken in the strict sense of the word and pious exercises on the one hand, and on the other all its conscious activities, we find that everything is offered up to God, not only formal prayer which is easily understood, but equally that which is not formal prayer, because it also is in accordance with the definition : " Prayer is the lifting up of the mind and soul to God."

Bossuet describes this secondary form of prayer : " It is the desire to praise God in all creatures and for all creatures by making the best use of them all and sanctifying them by using them so that he may be glorified : the good use of light and darkness, of fine weather and rain, of fire and ice ; the good use of all that exists and still more of myself, my eyes, my tongue, my mouth, my hands and feet, and my whole heart, and above all of my soul and my mind." [1]

In another place he says : " We must pray during the day, at night and as often as we awake ; and this continuous prayer does not consist in a perpetual tension of mind, but rather . . . having prayed at these different moments, the keeping of ourselves in a state of dependence upon God as far as is possible, showing

[1] Bossuet, *Letters*, vol. xxvii, p. 447.

him our needs—that is, silently laying them before him. Thus as the cracked parched earth by exposing her parched surface to the sky seems to be calling for rain, so the soul by exposing her wants to God appears to be saying: 'Lord, I have no need to pray to thee; my needs, my state of indigence speak for me.' Thus we pray without words, and God understands this language." [1]

A similar thought is expressed by a nun who writes: "I have always considered that during the night sleep is my best prayer. . . . Only, the whole of me is not sleeping, for my heart keeps watch by the tabernacle, and I ask my guardian angel to offer each heartbeat to our Lord as an act of love." [2]

St Augustine uses much the same idea in his explanation of the thirty-fourth Psalm to the Christians of Hippo: "If you are singing a hymn, you are praising God (always presupposing that you are thinking of the words). Then the hymn comes to an end, and it is time for a meal; if you keep yourself from over-eating you will be praising God. You go to your room to rest, and unless you get up with the set resolve to do something wrong, you will still be praising God. You go off to your business, and so long as there are no fraudulent dealings God will be praised. Are you a rural labourer? then be sure that there are no

[1] Bossuet, *Meditations on the Gospel*, vol. vi, pp. 61, 62.
[2] St Agnes of the Cross, 84.

weeds left in the ground you are digging, and once again this will be an occasion of praising God. Thus by the innocency of your works you will be praising God all the day long."

To sum up : prayer is every act that is offered up to the divine Majesty, to adore him, give thanks to him and implore his grace ; all is offered up to him, whether it be explicit formal prayer—that is, acts of prayer—or implicit virtual prayer, which includes all our supernaturalized activities, the fulfilment of our daily duties from a supernatural intention.

This truth can be expressed in another way : we can pray by thought and by will—by thought when we perform our spiritual exercises, or by the offering of our whole being and its activities to God, which implies that all our ordinary duties are performed from a supernatural motive.

The state of prayer is devotion to our daily duties.

II

The theory of this statement is clear, and the consequences are no less apparent. It would be a great mistake to imagine that although our life has been supernaturalized, yet because we are not always thinking of God, therefore we cannot be living in union with him. In the next chapter we shall see how it is possible and even highly desirable that work for God and thoughts of God should be intermingled. But before all it must clearly be understood that a supernatural life does not of necessity require the actual thought of God.

If this were the case, then only those acts which are explicitly a matter for prayer are capable of being offered to God, which would reduce our supernatural activities to acts of piety. It is quite evident that we cannot sit apart in some corner, with hands clasped, thinking about God, nor is it asked of us.

Sometimes, as has been seen already, formal prayer has to give way before a more pressing daily duty. Our daily duties come first, before everything else. True union with God consists in the union of the will with the will of God. If, after many careful and well-weighed considerations, I can honestly say that it is God's will I should pray, then it is my duty to pray. But if I am obliged to leave my prayers in order to attend to my duties, even if those duties are of such an absorbing nature that my mind cannot find a moment's respite in which to turn my thoughts to God, yet my union with him remains unbroken.

Sanctity is to be found in the union of the will with the will of God.

What is it that our Lord says of himself ? " My meat "—that is, the substance, the mainspring of my life—" is to do the will of him that sent me."[1] Mary, the most Christlike of all God's creatures, a Christian in the full sense of the word, answered the angel with the words: "Behold the handmaid of the Lord; be it done to me according to thy word."[2]

And we have nought else to do but to act in all things in accordance with the divine will. We are not called to imitate our Lord in his birth in the manger with the beasts, or in his death on the cross. We are asked to reproduce in our own lives his entire and radical submission in all things to the Father's will, which formed the foundation of his whole existence. The life of Christ consists essentially in this: he who is equal with his Father, made himself subordinate to him, so that by his obedience he could repair the first sin of disobedience. As the Word he is equal with his Father, as man he is inferior to him.

The purpose of his earthly life becomes more defined: "He humbled himself, becoming obedient unto death, even to the death of the cross."[3] Obedient unto death. For thirty years of his life he was subject. And the remainder of the time he was still obedient. "For Christ did not please himself";[4] he did not follow his own wishes in anything, for it would have meant that he was turning

---

[1] St John iv 34. [2] St Luke i 38.
[3] Phil. ii 8. [4] Rom. xv 3.

21

to his own use as man his activity which was centred in the Father. "Did you not know that I must be about my Father's business?"[1] He gave himself up to do his Father's business even to the tragedy of Gethsemani and Calvary. "Not my will but thine be done."[2] Up to the last moment of his earthly life, when ascending to his Father, he could say: "It is finished," I have accomplished the task.

We ought to be returning perpetually to this fundamental idea. Each one of us, in order to realize the Christian ideal, should have the same centre for his life as Christ in his human nature had for his, never taking our individual wishes for the end and object of our being, but on all occasions choosing more or less formally and always effectively the "things of God," God's will. Father Faber, in a note in his book *Bethlehem*, quotes a saying of Mary of Agreda, who declares our Lord revealed to her that he only exercised the power of choice on one occasion during his earthly life, and that was when he chose suffering.

If this is really "the Christ," every Christian, if he truly deserves to be called "another Christ," should make himself a replica, a copy of him who was supremely obedient and submissive to the wishes and desires of the Father, so that in all things he saw only the Father's will. "He hath sent me,"[3] said

[1] St Luke ii 49.   [2] *Ibid.*, xxii 42.
[3] Isa. lxi 1.

22

Isaias, in one of the most beautiful Messianic texts. Every Christian ought to reproduce in himself this ideal of the life of Christ.

To do this presupposes the death of our natural wishes, impulses, and desires. Self must be relegated to the background and not permitted to interfere in the ordering of our lives, or should be allowed only to make itself heard after God has spoken and always under his guidance. " I seek not my own will, but the will of him that sent me."[1] "For I do always the things that please him."[2] Thus self is reduced to a subject condition by this inner obedience which is the perfect imitation of our Lord. The same advice was given by St Paul to those who desired to reproduce in themselves the life of Christ crucified. To be crucified with Christ is not to drive the nails into our hands and feet, but to bend ourselves to this absolute self-renunciation which is like a living death.

To act for our own interests, by taking self as the ultimate aim, is not to accomplish an act that rises heavenwards, but on the contrary one that is decadent; it is to deflect to self, this mean petty self, some of our powers, taking self for the centre, and is a departure from the perfect imitation of Christ, whereby we cease to be united with the will of God, and give up prayer.

[1] St John v 30.   [2] *Ibid.*, viii 29.

It is almost superfluous to point out that this doctrine is simply the practical explanation of the foundations which St Ignatius lays down in his book of the *Exercises*, and which is given in the Catechism as the purpose of our existence: "to know, love, and serve God." Therefore my life, my being, and my powers should have only God for their last end. "In all that I have to do, there should be as little of self as possible," at any rate not self as the productive cause, for I never do over well that which I try and do by myself, nor self as my final objective. And this method of raising all my powers towards God, without any inter-mixture of self, is nothing less than a perfect prayer. It is the homage of all my life to him who has an absolute right to the supreme homage of all that exists. We see how St Ignatius in his book from the very first prepares the soul in the most solid manner for union with God.

The perfect prayer of the Church is the offering of the consecrated bread in the Mass. Now in the Host in place of the bread there is our Lord Jesus Christ; the substance of the bread is there no longer. In the same way my life will be a perfect prayer if there is no mingling of self-interest, if instead of self there is Christ, and I am entirely submissive to the will of God.

CHAPTER III

IT IS MOST PROFITABLE TO THINK OFTEN OF GOD

1. *The state of prayer is impossible without the habit of self-renunciation.*

2. *The habit of self-renunciation is impossible without constant recollection.*

I

LET us see how far we have got. We cannot always be thinking of God. Nor is it necessary. We can be constantly united with God without the constant thought of him. The union of the will with the will of God is the sole form of union that is really requisite.

Wherein, then, lies the utility of the exercise of the presence of God enjoined by all the masters of the spiritual life? We will now explain.

As has been said, it is necessary to have an absolutely pure intention in all our actions, so that the generous fulfilment of our daily duties may be directed towards the highest supernatural ideal. Thus our life, apart from moments of prayer, will be a prayerful life.

It is clear that the habit of giving an upward glance to God at the moment of action is a great assistance in aiding us to behave always with a pure intention and in freeing us from our natural impulses and fancies, so that, retaining our self-mastery, or rather, God becoming the sole Master, all our movements become dependent upon the Holy Spirit.

We see in the Gospel that whenever our Lord was about to undertake some important step, he always paused for a moment to raise his eyes to heaven, and only after this moment of recollection did he take up the work he had to do. " He lifted up his eyes to heaven " is a phrase which recurs with significant frequency. And doubtless when there was no outward sign of this prayer, there was the inward offering.

The ideal is the same for us. The constant subjection of self to the guidance of the Holy Spirit is made the easier from the fact of his presence in the soul, where he is asked explicitly to preside over all our doings. It is impossible to put the spirit of recollection into generous practice unless there is also a deeply rooted spirit of self-renunciation. We shall not submit whole-heartedly to the invisible Guest, unless he is kept in close proximity to us. The death of self cannot take place unless the spirit of life is already installed, unless it moves upon the face of the waters.

Man will not consent to drive away the money-changers from the temple of his soul until he realizes that it is a Holy of holies, not a house of traffic, but in very truth the house of God.

We thus reach two striking conclusions:

There can be no entire dependence upon the
guidance of the Holy Spirit, which is the true
meaning of living in Christ, without complete
self-renunciation. There cannot be
complete self-renunciation without the constant underlying spirit of faith, without the habit of
interior silence, a silence where God is
dwelling.

Many people do not see the connection
between thoughts about the King and the
service of the King; between the interior
silence which seems to consist in *immobility*
and the continual detachment which is the
essence of supreme *activity*.

If we look closer, it will be seen that there
is a strong, close, unbreakable link between
the two. Find a recollected person, and he
will be detached; seek one who is detached,
and he will be recollected. To have found the
one is to have discovered the other. The
truth of this may be estimated by the ease
with which the one *or* the other of these two
types can be found. Anyone who tries on
a given day to practise either recollection or
detachment, cannot ignore the fact that he is
doing a double stroke of work.

II

If the soul, in order to become fully Christlike, ought to live in entire dependence
upon the Holy Spirit, and if it is not possible
to live in complete dependence upon the Holy

Spirit unless the whole life is recollected, it is evident that recollection in the sense that has been explained already, constitutes one of the most precious virtues that can be acquired.

Father Pergmayer, one of those writers who has spoken most emphatically on this subject, does not hesitate to affirm that: " The shortest road to gain perfect love is to have God always present; sin is driven away, and the soul has no time to think of anything else or to complain and murmur. . . . The practice of the presence of God leads sooner or later to perfection."

Not to try and live in interior silence is equivalent to giving up the effort to lead a truly Christian life. The Christian life is a life of faith, lived in the invisible for what is invisible. Anyone who is not in constant contact with the invisible world, runs the risk of remaining always on the threshold of a true Christian life.

To quote the words of Father Gratry, " We must give up living in the outer and more superficial enclosure of the soul; we should go within and penetrate into its deepest recesses. And when we have arrived at this point, we must still go further in, until we reach the centre, which is no longer self, but God. There is the Master . . . and there it is that it may be vouchsafed us to abide with him for a whole day. Now once we have been permitted to pass a day with him, we

« Je sens que ma mission va commencer, ma mission de faire aimer le Bon Dieu comme je l'aime... de donner aux âmes ma petite voie de confiance et d'abandon. JE VEUX PASSER MON CIEL A FAIRE DU BIEN SUR LA TERRE. Ce n'est pas impossible, puisqu'au sein même de la vision béatifique les Anges veillent sur nous. Non, je ne pourrai prendre aucun repos jusqu'à la fin du monde. Mais lorsque l'Ange aura dit : « *Le temps n'est plus!* » alors je me reposerai, je pourrai jouir, parce que le nombre des élus sera complet. »

Ste Thérèse de l'Enfant-Jésus

PRIÈRE

en l'honneur de Ste Thérèse de l'Enfant-Jésus
et pour solliciter des grâces par son intercession

O Notre Père des Cieux, qui, par Ste Thérèse de l'Enfant-Jésus, voulez rappeler au monde l'amour miséricordieux qui remplit votre cœur, et la confiance filiale qu'on doit avoir en vous, nous vous remercions humblement d'avoir comblé de tant de gloire Celle qui fut toujours votre enfant si fidèle et de lui donner une puissance merveilleuse pour vous attirer chaque jour un très grand nombre d'âmes qui vous loueront éternellement.

Sainte Thérèse de l'Enfant-Jésus souvenez-vous de votre promesse de *faire du bien sur la terre*, répandez avec abondance votre *pluie de roses* sur ceux qui vous invoquent, et obtenez-nous de Dieu les grâces que nous attendons de sa bonté infinie.

Permis d'imprimer : † FRANÇOIS-MARIE
Évêque de Bayeux et Lisieux.

Les personnes qui reçoivent des grâces par l'intercession de Sainte Thérèse de l'Enfant-Jésus sont priées d'en communiquer le récit au Monastère des Carmélites de Lisieux (Calvados).

C. de L. pinxit

S^{TE} THÉRÈSE DE L'ENFANT-JÉSUS

« On n'a jamais trop de confiance dans le bon Dieu si puissant et si miséricordieux. »

Étoffe ayant touché aux reliques de la Sainte.

shall desire to follow him everywhere like his Apostles, his disciples, and his servants. Yea, Lord, when I have the privilege of spending the entire day with thee, I shall wish to follow thee always."[1]

Solitude is the stronghold of the strong. Strength is an active virtue, and our power of keeping silence marks the level of our capacity for action. "Without this interior cell, we should be incapable of doing great things either for ourselves or for others." The weak and unstable dislike to be alone. The majority of people look to amusement to save them from exerting themselves. They lose themselves in what is nought in order that self may not be lost in what is all. It was in the midst of the silence of the night that almighty God came to earth. "Silence," writes Father Faber, "has ever been as it were the luxury of great holiness. . . . So it is the first life which he, the eternally silent-spoken Word of the Father, chooses for himself. All his after-life was coloured by it. In his childhood he let speech seem to come slowly to him, as if he were acquiring it like others, so that under this disguise he might prolong his silence, delaying thus even his colloquies with Mary. Mary also herself, and Joseph, caught from him, as by a heavenly contagion, a beautiful taciturnity. In his eighteen years of hidden life, silence still prevailed in the holy house of Nazareth.

---

[1] *Meditations*, pp. 149, 150.

Words, infrequent and brief, trembled in the air, like music which was too sweet for one strain to efface another, while the first still vibrated in the listening ear. In the three years' ministry, which was given up to talking and teaching, he spoke as a silent man would speak, or like a God making revelations. Then in his Passion, when he had to teach by his beautiful way of suffering, silence came back again, just as an old habit returns at death, and became once more a characteristic feature of his life." [1] We think so much of appearances that we are unable to appreciate anything that does not appeal to the senses. Silence is the source whence springs effectual effort. The jet of water is forced silently to bore its way through the stone before it is able to burst forth bubbling into song.

It must be well understood that when silence is recommended, it is interior silence that is meant, which should be imposed upon the senses and imagination to avoid the liability of being taken out of ourselves in spite of ourselves at every moment. If the oven door is perpetually kept open, to adopt the simile used by St Teresa, the heat will escape. It takes a long while to raise the temperature, but a second is sufficient for it to run down. A crack in the wall will let in the icy outer air, and the whole process has to be begun again.

[1] *Bethlehem*, ii, pp. 74, 75.

· fortitude ·

CONSUMING
FIRE

DESCEND WITHIN
ME
REPRODUCE IN ME
ANOTHER INCAR-
NATION OF THE
WORD
THAT I MAY BE TO HIM
A NEW HUMANITY
WHEREIN HE CAN
RENEW HIS
MYSTERY

An excellent method of preserving interior silence is to keep silence without. This is the reason for the cloister and the grill. But, even in the world, each one of us can make his own solitude, a boundary beyond which nothing can force its way unperceived.

It is not noise in itself which is the difficulty, but noise that is pointless ; it is not every conversation, but useless conversations ; not all kinds of occupation, but aimless occupations. In point of fact, everything that does not serve some good purpose is harmful. It is foolish, nay, more, it is a betrayal, to devote to a useless objective powers that can be given to what is essential.

There are two ways of separating ourselves from almighty God, quite different one from the other, but both disastrous, though for different reasons : mortal sin and voluntary distractions ; mortal sin which objectively breaks off our union with God, and voluntary distractions which subjectively interrupt or hinder our union from being as close as it ought to be. We should speak only when it is preferable not to keep silence. The Gospel does not say merely that we shall have to give an account of every evil word, but of every *idle* thought.

We must speed up our lives, as modern people express it, and get rid of everything that lessens the output ; the spiritual life more than anything else requires this speeding up, for it is the most important. The interest which the majority of people take in things of no account—the noises in the street, the behaviour of the passers-by, the flagrant emptyheadedness of the daily papers whether intentional or unintentional—is almost incredible. What a joy it would be if suddenly, by some unexpected good fortune, everything in the world that does not serve some good purpose were to come to an end; if those who have nothing to say were to keep silence, this life would be a paradise! The cloister is what it is because there men and women learn how to keep silence. They do not always succeed, but at least they are learning, and that is a great thing. Elsewhere it is a lesson that is not even learned. Yet speech is a great art, and conversation a valuable pastime, perhaps the most precious in existence, but good use is not abuse. It is customary on the anniversary of the Armistice to keep a two minutes' silence: this silence is in memory of the victory of the Allied troops. If the world would learn how to keep silence, this practice of recollection would lead to many victories.

" If any man offend not in word, the same is a perfect man." "And let every man be swift to hear, but slow to speak." [1]

Our usual habit is to behave in an exactly contrary manner. Everyone talks, no one

---

[1] St Jas. iii 2; *ibid.*, i 19.

listens, least of all to him who most deserves to be heard, the interior Master. There are few perfect souls because there are few lovers of silence. Silence is the equal of perfection, not in all, but in a great many instances. Put it to the test—it is worth the trouble—and the result will be a revelation.

PART II
THE PRACTICAL SIDE

CHAPTER IV

HOW TO PRAY WELL

1. *Preparation for prayer.*

2. *The need of action in prayer.*

3. *Perseverance in prayer.*

A FICTION that must be destroyed is that it is difficult to pray. Nothing is more simple, so long as we know how to set about it. No one wishes to deny the difficulties of prayer—difficulties for the most commonplace minds, as well as for more elevated souls. This modest little volume is not meant for the latter; it will suffice to send them to read the dramatic pages of St John of the Cross, where the laborious and successive stages whereby the soul is purified from earthly attachments are described by one who has the authority of a saint, and who has himself passed through each one of these stages, in which Mount Calvary is a close neighbour to Mount Tabor.

There remain, therefore, the difficulties experienced by ordinary people. They are due in the majority of cases to the lack of *method* in our mode of coming into contact with the supernatural world, to want of *courage* in exerting ourselves during prayer, or to failure to *persevere* in the presence of God in times of aridity, when sensible consolations are absent.

We must learn—

How to prepare for prayer.

How to be active during prayer.

How to persevere in prayer.

All the technique of prayer can be deduced from putting these three injunctions into practice.

I

PREPARATION FOR PRAYER

In the preceding pages, care has been taken to distinguish between two different forms of recollection : the one due to the bounty of God, and the other the result of our own efforts, coupled with the habitual grace of God.

It is clear that in the first case, granted that God does everything, human activity will be reduced to the minimum. All that is requisite is that we shall hold in reserve some subject of converse with our Lord, in case he should cease from entertaining us himself. It would be an interruption and a hindrance to try and interpolate our own reflections or queries when the Holy Spirit is making his communications to us. We are already in contact with God; what is the sense of behaving as if we had to use our own efforts to approach him ? Who would turn on the electric light when the sun is shining ?

Let the soul remain tranquil and listen ; that is the rule to be followed, though this does not imply inactivity.

Quite different is the type of recollection which is the outcome of our own exertions. God is close by, but hidden as is his custom. He waits to reveal himself until we shall ourselves pierce the veil which conceals him.

To kneel down and then wait, without doing anything, would be often a clear loss of time. Heaven helps those who help themselves.

How can we help ourselves ? In this manner.

Let us imagine that the mind is either full of distractions or quite empty. We have got to introduce into its field of vision something that will induce it to think about these invisible realities. This will be either an abstract idea, a concrete fact, or some text.

An *idea*.—Let us take the idea of death. I have a memory, an intelligence, and a will. I will bring these three faculties to bear upon this idea. *Memory* (which includes the imagination).—I will try and recall to mind all that I know about death, its circumstances, its sudden unexpected appearance, and represent to myself a death-bed scene, as a whole and in detail. *Intelligence*.—Man must die. Then *I* also shall have to die. Am I mortal or not? Yes, I am. Then I shall die, I who at this present moment am so full of life. *Will*.— Since I must die, I ought to live with the thought of death ever before me, and detach myself from all earthly things. Can I say that I am detached?

This is merely one example; a thousand others will suggest themselves, and in every case the method is the same.

This is not some ingenious artificial method; the mode of procedure, if procedure it may be termed, is one that is common to every reasonable human being, when he reflects. He tries to remember some incident, and weaves into one whole, by a process of induction or deduction, the data which his memory provides, and, in consequence of them, decides as his reason orders him to do.[1]

To complain of the technique of prayer is to forget that although the faculty of speech is quite a simple matter, yet to explain how the vowels and consonants should be pronounced is not so easy. The theory of warfare is complicated, the use of firearms is simple.

This form of prayer is called meditation. The word here is applied in its exact signi-

[1] St Ignatius calls this method the Exercise of the Three Powers.

ficance, for the term can be used in a wider sense, to include all the general methods of treating with God, and as a synonym for prayer. We may say we are going to make our meditation, and not mean thereby the exclusive use of the exercise of the Three Powers, but any form of mental prayer.

One of these forms is called contemplation; here also the word is used in its restricted sense, for in its full significance it implies the type of prayer adopted by lofty souls. Contemplation, as St Ignatius understood it, is the setting the mind to work, not upon an idea, but upon a fact.

Let us take the Annunciation, or some other incident in the life of our Lady. To avoid being overburdened at the outset, it is a good plan to divide the mystery into the beginning, the middle, and the end, or rather, before, during, and after. In each part we can take as the framework the persons, words, and actions.

THE ANNUNCIATION—At the beginning (that is, before the appearance of the angel). *Persons.* —There is only one, Mary. I look at her, and first of all I notice her general appearance, her attitude of recollection. Then I go into more details; I consider her features, her eyes, her hands, etc. This is not difficult. Next I look within at her thoughts, her affections With the assistance of this easy method, who is there who is not capable of penetrating into the hidden meaning of the mystery?

Words.—There are none I listen and drink in the silence. God does not make himself known in the tumult: have I not experienced this in my own case?

Actions.—There are none.

This can be continued for as long as is necessary. The second point is the coming of the angel Gabriel; here there will be words to be listened to; I take them one by one and weigh them.

Let us give this method a fair trial and set to work conscientiously and not give it up after the first attempt. I will guarantee that if our converse with God is prepared beforehand and we have the courage to persevere, we shall find prayer no longer hard. There are difficulties in prayer, but they do not lie here. To contemplate only means to look at something or someone. We know what it means to use our eyes. Then open them wide. The obscure world of faith is more luminous than we imagine: it is only necessary to wish to see.

I can make use of a concrete *fact* or an abstract *idea* as a means of approaching God in prayer. Or I can take a *text*, a psalm, or a well-known prayer, the meaning of which I wish to recall to mind, a verse of the *Imitation*. Those who wish to penetrate deeply into the mystery of God within us, can make use of a little book somewhat resembling the *Imitation* entitled *Vivre en Dieu*.[1]

This manner of prayer is excellent for beginners, and also for those who are tired; it is good for everybody, provided they cease using a book directly a thought or loving aspiration comes to them. Many persons who practise meditation come to prayer without having prepared for it: this, as we have said before, is a psychological error. It is more, it is an indelicacy. I am about to hold converse with *God;* it is important to emphasize this fact. With the Lord of all. Imagine that an important personage is coming to visit a city. Do you think that those whose business it is to receive him would say: "It is quite futile to make any preparations beforehand; we shall get through all right"? Apply these words to the case we are considering; they are far more appropriate.

II

THE NEED OF ACTION IN PRAYER

Even when we have prepared both ourselves and our subject for prayer, it must not be imagined that the simple fact of kneeling down at our prayer-desk will instantly reveal to us the treasures of the supernatural world; pearls cannot be purchased for a few half-

[1] Bureau of the Apostleship of Prayer, 9, rue de Montplaisir, Toulouse, 2 francs 50.

pence. We must devise means, use our brains, exert ourselves. The name pious *exercises* is very apt, and it was St Ignatius, a keen observer, who called his book on Christian perfection the *Spiritual Exercises*.

In point of fact, very few persons really *exert* themselves—that is, force themselves to take pains during prayer. To "make our meditation" is, for many of us, to go over the exciting or soporific considerations of some writer in a more or less passive manner.

There are some good books of meditation in existence, but they are not numerous. Often the theme is over-elaborate and drawn out, and written in a complicated and too literary style; sometimes it is too difficult and abstract, or is expressed in a wealth of theological terms that is unattractive and gives an air of being archaic and unreal. Therefore some persons will say: "If my meditation has to consist in dissertations of this kind, I prefer to give it up immediately, I shall never succeed."

Perhaps this reasoning is too severe; yet it must be recognized that certain manuals of meditation have, in part at any rate, contributed to give this false impression of mental prayer, and so spread the notion that it is something repellent, impractical, and far-fetched. Such an idea of prayer is far removed from the definition given by St Teresa, "Prayer is a loving converse with

God," or the answer made to St John Vianney, the Curé, " I look at him, and he looks at me." [1]

Our advice is that a book of meditations should not be used unless there is really no alternative. The reason for the difficulty is not that they are badly written, but because they contain someone else's thoughts, and are not suited to our individual needs. There is nothing more personal than prayer. You say that the sentiments suggested to you by this writer mean nothing to you, and I can readily believe it : they are his own ideas and do not necessarily correspond with your mentality. Why, when you are meditating, should you use the thoughts and sentiments of someone else for the development of your subject ? He may have good ideas. But they are not *yours*. Why not try and draw them out for yourself as he has drawn them out for himself ? His ideas may very probably have done good to him, but they have only a distant connection with you and the needs of your soul. If after having conscientiously tried to make use of your own powers you can find nothing, then you cannot do better than call upon someone else's ideas. But, please, give yourself full credit first, and try and produce from your own store that which you are wishing to say to God.

[1] Someone asked the Curé d'Ars for a definition of faith. The reply was : " It is speaking to God as if he were our fellow-man."

The child who wants to speak to his mother does not first hasten into the library to look for a guide to conversation or a collection of polite speeches. No, he has his own little phrases, his smiles and caresses, and the mother is far more pleased with these prattlings than she would have been with the fine but unreal expressions in the printed book.

When we speak to God it is not in the language of Bossuet, nor is it necessary. But if we put our heart into our prayers, our poor words will certainly find their way to God. And how much greater the profit to ourselves!

The subject-matter of our meditations, apart from certain variations, is the mysteries of our Lord's life throughout the year taken in conjunction with the liturgical cycle of feasts. It is therefore a good plan to provide ourselves with a book of the Gospels as a foundation for prayer. Among many other books, there is one by Canon Weber, *Les Quatre Évangiles dans un seul*,[1] which is brought out in several convenient forms that take very little room. The volume has the advantage that it gives the life of our Lord from the Gospels, in one connected whole, without the repetition to be found from reading the Gospels separately; the different parts and the episodes in each are clearly divided.

[1] *The Saint Évangile*, by le Chanoine A. Weber (Œuvre de la Diffusion du Saint Évangile, Verdun).

With this slender volume as a basis, and by making use of one or other of the methods indicated in the preceding paragraph, it is very easy, after a little practice, to make our meditation. If it is an *idea* that is under consideration, then the exercise of the Three Powers will be used; if an *historical event*, then the contemplative method; if a *text*, then a more or less searching or rapid working out of this or that saying of our Lord's. Here, it seems, is all that is required for the making of a good meditation, provided we are determined to take an active part in it and not to remain passive. There is no desire to be over-exclusive in suggesting the life of our Lord as the subject for meditation throughout the year; it is the advice of the masters of the spiritual life. Some persons will like to take some word or thought from the Mass of the day, or a psalm, etc. Any subject is good that serves to nourish the soul, every method is of use if thereby good results are obtained.

It should be noted that activity in prayer does not mean to become an automaton, a mere piece of mechanism. That some persons through over-respect for method will sooner go through the treadmill than allow the Holy Spirit free play in their souls, is not a proof that methods are of no use, but rather that there are clumsy people in the world. The value of a thing must not be judged by its abuse.

It is quite clear that having carefully prepared the subject for prayer, which out of
deference to the divine Master we ought to do,
if our Lord chooses to substitute another
subject for the one we have selected, the rule
is to adapt ourselves to the inspiration from
on high, and not to cling to our own choice,
whatever it may cost us to give it up. A
subject that is self-chosen must always give
place to one which it pleases the Master of
the soul to suggest, and which in his estima-
tion is preferable. We should always follow
the leading of the Holy Spirit, nor should we
venture to impose upon him our own ideas.

Our activity in this case consists, not in
awkwardly trying to insert our own phrases
into the conversation, but in leaving free scope
for the lesson which God is desirous of giving.
Our efforts will be spent in repressing an ill-
advised activity. We shall show our activity
not so much by speech as in listening.
There are chatterers in prayer as elsewhere;
let us avoid it. If it pleases our Lord to
instruct the soul in a more or less direct
manner and without troubling about our preparations, let us not in any way hinder his
action. All we have to do is to intensify our
interior silence so as to give him the opportunity of making quite clear all that he wishes
to say. "You make the river-bed," said our
Lord to a Visitation nun, "and I will be the
torrent."[1] To St Margaret Mary he said:

[1] Mère Marie Ponnet, of the Convent of the Visitation of Vaissieux.

" Place yourself in my presence as if you were a bare canvas." These words, " make," and " place yourself," imply a form of passiveness that is singularly active.

To sum up : When the Holy Spirit leaves us to our own devices, then we can make use of our own resources. When, on the other hand, he shows that he wishes to dispense with our own actions, then we ought to place ourselves humbly at his disposition and as generously as possible bend ourselves to his designs.

III

PERSEVERANCE IN PRAYER

Two important conditions for success in prayer may be said to have been fulfilled. We have made up our minds to prepare for prayer and to exert ourselves during prayer.

It remains for us to persevere.

The soul is subject to the same weather variations as the body. The sun is not always shining brightly. Many dull days may be counted upon, without mentioning periodical returns of darkness. Let us distinguish between three types of prayer : consolation in prayer, desolation, and passive prayer. When God sends consolations, there is nothing easier than to persevere in prayer ; therefore it is unnecessary to waste time upon this point. But there are certain pitfalls that ought to be pointed out, which, although they would not lead us to abandon prayer, would lessen the value of it.

The first is to mistake sensible consolations for the true mystic touch of infused recollection, and to imagine that because we have experienced sensible sweetness in prayer, therefore we have been favoured with mystical graces. The advice given by St John of the Cross is applicable to this case. After saying that the soul should " never separate herself from her loving attention to God," an injunction which does not touch upon this subject, he adds words which are strikingly applicable : " But never desire to obtain any extraordinary graces."

Does this mean that we ought not to long for the closest union with God ? Certainly we ought to do so. But, to adopt the division made by the theologians, it is one thing to wish an ever-increasing fullness of sanctifying grace, which is always highly desirable, and quite another to desire visions, revelations, free gifts, and most imprudent. St John of the Cross evidently alludes to these last in his words.

In general, souls to whom these mystical favours have been vouchsafed are far from desiring them, above all at the outset. They are alarmed by them. An expert director, if he perceives solid piety and the signs of true mysticism, has to instil confidence into the soul. The union of these two elements is both less uncommon than certain rigorous minds will allow, and less frequent than other optimists imagine.

Another danger in sensible consolations is to think that because we are content, therefore God is pleased with us.

Yesterday we were struggling with besetting distractions and we fought bravely against them. When we rose from prayer, there was not much enthusiasm left. To-day we were in the seventh heaven, all went well from first to last and without much effort. God did everything. It would be childish to conclude that the meditation of to-day is much superior to that of yesterday. In reality, the value of a meditation may be gauged by the intensity of charity shown at the moment, and it is quite possible that when we were struggling against distractions yesterday, there was more charity at work than to-day when favours were received. In theory, merit is not measured by the amount of effort expended, but by the exercise of charity.

Father Lancicius states very clearly : "It is an unpermissible scruple to accuse oneself of having made a bad meditation because we were unable to feel any pious affections." According to him, the following examples are deserving of censure :

"If idle thoughts before meditation are not repulsed "—which presupposes that the meditation is made soon after rising. "If, during meditation, distractions are not driven away at the first warning of conscience. If meditation is not continued for the time allotted to it. If our attitude is not sufficiently respectful, so that we should be ashamed if suddenly surprised by some spiritually-minded person. If the eyes are allowed to look about at what is going on, or the ears to listen to what is being said." And he concludes with the words: "Apart from these instances, the meditation is always good"—words which will act as a stimulus to the zeal of some persons, and calm the anxieties of others.

In addition to these times of consolation, periods of desolation must be reckoned with. This is the stumbling-block to the majority of fervent souls.

It is necessary to know the methods that God usually employs when he raises the soul to the way of perfection. At the commencement he loads it with favours. This is in order to give it an idea of what he is, to free it from the bondage of the visible world, and to enable it to appreciate the invisible world. He is lavish with his favours, and draws it to him with many consolations, and sets it on fire with burning love and the longing to continue the converse that has been interrupted. The soul feels the attraction. And how should it not be glad to be in such sweet company? The words of St Peter on the mount of the Transfiguration rise spontaneously to our lips : " Master, it is good for us be here." [1]

Then suddenly everything changes. Sensible devotion in prayer, after having lasted for a long or short period of time, comes to an end, —in some cases suddenly, in others more gradually. The brilliant sunshine is followed by a kind of night, which is all the more dense because of the radiant sunlight which went before. The impression given is of someone passing from broad daylight into a tunnel or underground cellar.

Here it is that God is waiting. Some persons—and they are the larger number—lose heart, for they are less truly pious than they appeared to be, and were following God more for his favours than for himself; therefore, now that prayer is no longer a delight, they abandon everything. They believe themselves to be generous, and perhaps others think they are ; but, in part at any rate, they are unconsciously selfish. They were not seeking God, but themselves.

Now it is God's wish that we should—if we may venture to use the expression—look not at his hands, but at his heart, not at what he gives, but at what he is. This is why on occasion he withdraws his sensible attractions and leaves us to the exercise of pure faith. He wishes to discover whether the soul is truly seeking for him, or for his benefits. God

[1] St Luke ix 33.

desires to dwell alone in the soul. He wishes to be loved for himself, and so, sooner or later, he withdraws everything when he vouchsafes to raise it to higher stages of prayer, so that it may dwell *solitary with him alone*. Hence these strange purifying experiences, both active and passive (the night of the soul and the night of the senses), through which God leads it. His aim is to reach down until there is nothing in the soul but himself. When pious writers refer to the solitude of God in the soul, they are alluding to this divine urgency. Happy those of us whose generosity and ardour is strong enough to enable them to direct their lives towards this end, and who persevere unwearied in spite of periods of spiritual dryness and of desolation, that are sometimes of a strangely dramatic character. But we must clearly realize the line of demarcation that divides the truly interior soul from the pious dilettante who only exerts himself when it suits him. If among the readers of these pages there are any who at this moment are struggling in the dark night, beside our Lord in his agony in the Garden of Gethsemani, let them understand that upon their perseverance depends the bestowal of graces, whose value they ignore, whence they will obtain a sanctified power of energy that will surpass their strongest hopes.

It remains to say a word about the prayer of quiet. To persevere in this apparently requires less effort than in the prayer of desolation. But in reality it demands more energy. The reason for this lies in the fact that unless the spirit of faith is very strong in us, the supernatural life does not attract us, and to pray means to endeavour to come into contact with the invisible world.

To reach the invisible, or even merely to go in search of it, necessitates the breaking away from outward appearances and the pleasures of sense. When Moses went to find God on Mount Sinai, he left his sandals at the foot, and laboriously climbed up out of the plain. To climb alarms us; we like the flat ground, and prefer to walk comfortably shod. How many persons are there who, if they were truthful with themselves, would have to cast away their sandals!

But let us consider the case of a really generous person. A difficulty of quite another order threatens to paralyze his loving transports. He longs to make acts of adoration, praise, and thanksgiving: maybe it is his greatest desire. But with what can he give praise or adore? He has nothing, for he is poverty itself. How can his feeble prayers ever attain to what is due to the infinite God? What has he that can be offered to God, that is worth anything, and is not almost an insult? God is the great God, and he is only a creature. How dare he come into the presence of him who is all in all? It is the struggle between Jacob and the angel; the soul is vanquished at the outset, the angel is always victorious.

Too many people when they pray do not make use of their intelligence, or, if we prefer, we can say instead that they show by their prayers they have not fully grasped what St Paul calls the Christian mystery, the mystery of our incorporation with our Saviour Jesus Christ in the unity of one mystical body. "I am the vine, you are the branches." [1] There is no difficulty for those who realize this great truth. If I had to love God and give him praise by myself, or with my own powers, I should be quite incapable of it, and my acts of homage before ever they left this plane would be forced to acknowledge their powerlessness. But I am not asked to do this. Only our Lord Jesus Christ is capable of offering to the Father the glory which is his due, and owing to a wonderful act of mercy, I am one with Jesus Christ. Not only has our Lord made himself one with us in order to redeem us, but he has vouchsafed also to make each one of us a part of himself. This is the meaning of these words: no longer have I to love with my own powers, for I have at my disposal, when I pray, the prayer of our Lord. Jesus does not wish to be complete without me; he has made me an integral part of himself. My prayer is

[1] St John xv 5.

insignificant and beneath everything; but his prayer is mine, I am able to make use of it, nay, more, it is my duty to use it.

In Baptism I received the power of offering our Lord to his Father, not on behalf of all the faithful, for only the sacrament of Ordination confers this, but on my own account. In this consists the spiritual priesthood of which St Peter speaks, an office so lofty that he, the first pope, does not hesitate to call it "a kingly priesthood." [1] Some people do not like this title to be applied to the ordinary lay man or woman, but there is no reason to be afraid of it—we should try and understand what it means. It is a grand word and expresses a great truth.

To pray as a Christian, to use this term in its strict sense, is to pray after the manner of the Church, who every time that she prays, by virtue of our baptismal priesthood, makes oblation of Christ to his Father. There is too much self in the majority of our prayers— not that our goodwill can ever err in over-generosity, or that the offering of our whole self is not always ardently desired by God— but that there is too much of self in the sense that there is not enough of Jesus Christ in our offering.

We speak of heaven and earth. But this is not correct. We have forgotten that there

---

[1] 1 St Pet. ii 9.

E

is a third factor. There is heaven and earth, and, between the two, Jesus, the Mediator, with whom we are one. The right expression for our relations with God in prayer is to be found in the words of St Paul: "Your life is hid with Christ in God."[1] Here are the three—God, Christ, and ourselves—with their relative value: we are nothing, yet it is for us to pour the drop of water into the chalice, which reminds us of our exact place as merely a drop of water; Christ, ever making mediation, which rises to the Father, for the glory of the Father and the redemption of the world; and above all God, the Holy Trinity, to whom be all glory and honour. It is the "*by whom, with whom, and in whom,*" of the Mass. There is not sufficient of Jesus Christ in our prayer as "other Christs."

"Self must be forgotten completely," advises Father Guilloré; and these words, after what has been said already, are not in danger of being misinterpreted. "You should only look two ways, one way towards the divine operations of our Lord, which you have in your hands like a present, and the other towards the Father to whom it is being offered up. This is the meaning of 'putting on Christ.'"

"I can no longer keep my eyes on myself," writes one who fully understood the meaning of living in Christ. "I do not mean that I am

[1] Col. iii 3.

no longer conscious of my miseries; on the contrary, it is only the experience of my frequent falls that has taught me fully to realize them. But what is that, what is this nothingness in comparison with the infinity of God? It seems to me that to stop there [1] is to insult our Lord, who has paid the debt, and whose merits we have acquired. If I had not Christ with me, I should never venture to approach the Father, but with Christ as my support, and clothed with him, I dare everything, for I am rich with all his riches."

[1] It must not be imagined that she made her union with our Lord an excuse for not combating her faults. We are a hundred leagues from this teaching of Luther and the *pecca fortiter et crede fortius.*

CHAPTER V

TO TURN EVERYTHING INTO PRAYER

1. *Purity of intention.*

2. *The perfecting of our actions.*

WE have seen that in order to remain in a *state* of prayer it is not necessary to be always actively praying.

Every action done for God rises to his throne as an act of homage. It constitutes a lifting up of our whole being to his supreme Majesty, a recognition which, though not always explicit, is none the less real, of his sovereign due, and is the filial act of the creature offering everything to his Creator and his Father. In practice, what is required of one who wishes to "pray always"? He must give to each one of his intentions the maximum of supernatural perfection that is humanly possible. And in this he will be aided greatly if he tries to perform his actions with the maximum professional skill of which he is humanly capable.

In other words, he has to purify the underlying motives of his actions, and to do his best under all circumstances.

I

PURITY OF INTENTION

We do not think sufficiently of the goodness of God in the mechanism of the doctrine of intention.

When we reflect upon the pettiness of our habitual actions and the feeble result they produce, we are alarmed. How do we spend the twenty-four hours of the day? In extraordinarily hackneyed actions. Eight hours or more in bed, one or two in feeding, and what about the rest of the time? Even in the case of persons whose work is of a more exalted character—the artist, writer, poet—what is the value of their masterpieces in the sight of God, and how much of their time is spent in duties other than artistic labours and creative work? There are proofs to be corrected, publishing accounts to be reckoned, and other things. How is it possible to amass eternal merit with such trifles as the sweeping of a room for the mother of a family, or the cooking for a general servant, for a classical master the explanation fifteen times repeated of a passage from Cæsar or Virgil?

If a supernatural intention is introduced into the actions, large or small, of daily life, it is as if leaven had been added, for immediately they begin to have life and to rise heavenward. A hidden fermentation is working in them. They have been changed from insignificant detail, into eloquent praise-offerings to almighty God. That which was a lifeless atom is now a living poem. Henceforward nothing is base or vile; the poet's verse, the sauce for the luncheon, the speculative theorizing at the Sorbonne University, or a bundle of posts standing in a corner of the carpenter's workshop—all these can be supernaturalized. And how is this miracle to be accomplished? By the intention.

We should indeed be unfortunate if God were to judge our acts on their own merit. It is only the privileged few who are permitted to do great things. We shall be judged by the motive of our actions; and what a consoling thought it is to know that an unimportant existence, inspired by high motives, is incomparably greater than that which the world calls a noble life, but which is only paved with petty motives. The whole of man is in the will which lies behind the thoughts and affections, and not in the broom, the brush, or the pen. Happy is the life beyond the veil where true values will be made plain; there it will be manifested to all men that those personages who performed startling deeds are nothing but gas-bags, while the woman pointed out by St Francis of Assisi to Brother Juniper, surpasses in supernatural dignity the lukewarm monk or nun.

It is not sufficient to admire the beauty of a good intention, we must realize the difficulties in the way.

The greater number of our motives are "mixed." The case of the evil-doer, who seeks to do wrong, may be laid aside. Here we are speaking of the good Christian, the fervent soul. There is no doubt that they are searching for God. But not God alone —it is God with the addition of some whim, some satisfaction of self-love, or the desire of well-being or of vanity.

The *Imitation* recommends us to have a "*simple eye* that aims at nothing but God," [1] —that is to say, an exclusively supernatural aim, which the multiplicity of human motives cannot alter or disturb. St Ignatius proposes the same ideal to his sons in the words : " That in all things they may seek God, and God alone." We have here a counsel given by all the masters of the spiritual life, and one of which we should remind ourselves continually.

Man belittles everything with which he comes into contact. He is made of spirit and matter, and this dual characteristic makes itself visible in all that he touches. He is born of two parents and seems to have a mania for what is complex. We should keep a watch over this habit, and frequently examine the motives of our actions and purity of intention. The author of the book *Paraitre* describes someone whose perpetual preoccupation was to " think of him-

---

[1] *Imitation*, Book III, chap. xxxi.

self." What others are thinking, what they
will say, or maybe what they might say—if
we could only realize how little, as a general
rule, others think about us, and still more
how lacking in interest are their opinions,
and how little deserving to influence us!
The greater number of human beings are led
by shadows. Let us cast a strong light upon
them. For whom and for what object am I
doing this? To win a smile of approval from
Jack or Peter, for the probable approbation
of Mrs. So-and-so, which often never comes
off. Be done with it!

In certain cases it is wise, before an action,
to make a determined effort to get rid of this
complexity, if it exists, so as gradually to
succeed in suppressing it quite naturally on
every occasion. But it is better still to get
into the habit of acting from the highest
motive that is apparent. There is some
work that I have to do. It can be done
either because it is my duty and the will of
God—and this is a perfect motive—or because
it is a means of assuring my position, and
of enabling me to provide suitably for my
family—also an excellent motive, but of a
natural order and greatly inferior to the
former, which was wholly supernatural—or,
thirdly, because it makes people think well of
me, and gives me the opportunity of shining
in the public eye—and this is a far less
honourable motive—and so on. It must not
be thought that all is lost because a lower

motive may have intervened during the course of the action.

Clearly, if it is a case of a manifestly bad intention which entirely swallows up the former good intention so as completely to destroy it (we must note these two conditions), the result will be a bad action, and the gravity of this is to be ascertained according to the ordinary moral laws affecting sin.

But more often the former intention remains. I give alms out of compassion and charity; the secondary intention that glides in is that others may see me, for example, but it does not totally destroy it, though it alters it a little by adding a purely human element to an act which at the first was entirely supernatural. The action remains good, only the merit is somewhat diminished by the intrusion of a less noble motive; the simplest method of getting over it is to address this upsetting underhand intruder in the words of St Bernard : " I did not begin this for you, and I have no intention of finishing it for you."

II

THE PERFECTING OF OUR ACTIONS

The normal accompaniment of a perfect intention is the perfecting of our actions to do our best as in the sight of God. If the complaints heard on all sides are to be believed, actions that are well done are becoming rare. A trade conscience is disappearing. Men do not work; they avoid it. There is no longer, as formerly, the same degree of solicitude to do "the best possible." Péguy, in his book *L'Argen*, speaks thus on this subject: "We have known this painstaking love of perfection to be shown both in the mass and in the smallest detail, and this pious craze for the 'task well done' maintained and extended to its utmost limit. During my childhood at my home, I have seen the people re-caning chairs as carefully and exactly as their forefathers used to cut building stones for the cathedrals. . . . Take note that nowadays it does not really please the workmen to do nothing: they would prefer to work. They hear the call of their race, and their hands are aching to be busy. . . . But their clever leaders have explained to them that this is socialism, and that is revolution."

Can it be said of us Christians that the pagan influence of the world in which we live, the habit of taking things as they come, has not penetrated somewhat into our lives?

What kind of professional conscience has each one of us in our state of life? How do we fulfil our daily duties? Is the work that has to be carried through done as well as we are capable of doing it? If not, what can we expect? Because our Master is good and rewards the smallest act even when only half finished, shall we be content only to give him acts that are not complete, a portion of our labour and half the produce of our undertakings ?

We often long that our lives might be different. We should like them to be full of other events and to have a varied career, that our home duties should be less monotonous and of a more startling character. It is no secret that no one is content with his lot. He would like to change places with his neighbour. Now God does not ask us to do something _different_, but to do what has to be done _differently_. Not to change our daily actions, but the manner in which we perform them. To darn the linen or correct an exercise, if it is part of our duty, merits a heavenly reward. Again, there is the way our work is done. Each one of us, if he carefully examines his conscience, will discover that on many occasions he slacks or even goes on strike. The saints did not behave in this manner. Whatever had to be done they did, and here is the most elementary as well as the most profound mark of sanctity. Some of them accomplished great things ; but they did not become saints for that reason, and were only permitted to do great deeds as a reward for fidelity in small things. There are many among the blessed, like St John Berchmans, who are honoured precisely because in a short life they realized perfection in their ordinary actions. One who was asked his opinion of Father Chevrier, the evangelist of Marseilles, replied: "I know nothing about him except that he always keeps his door shut." The answer was made half jokingly, but it was expressive, for it implied complete self-control and fidelity in small things. To live a life of uninterrupted prayer that will beautify the grey monotony of our daily duties—who is there who could not become a saint in this way?

The great secret of a fervent life is to take as our ideal the maxim: "Act on all occasions as our Lord would have acted, had he been in our place."[1] And it is to be noted that this is not an imaginary situation, more or less fictitious, but a reality. Each one of us in a state of grace is a living member of Christ, and therefore the acts we perform from a supernatural motive, Christ, as head of the human race, accomplishes in us and by us.

How would Christ fulfil this humble detail of my life? I must do it in the same manner. And this other thing, and that? If we adopt this counsel as the practical guide of our lives, we shall not need to look elsewhere for the road to sanctity; it is found already, and there is no more rapid or efficacious method.

[1] R. Plus, *In Christ Jesus*.

CHAPTER VI

TO SPREAD ABROAD THE SPIRIT OF PRAYER

1. *The practice of ejaculatory prayer.*

2. *The advantages of this practice.*

To take trouble over our prayers, and to make our whole existence in to a life of prayer, these are the requisite conditions for a true and close union with God.

To these two points must be added a third, which is to make as many aspirations to God as possible during the course of the day. This is the habit of ejaculatory prayer. We shall see how this practice is to be carried out and what are its advantages.

I

THE PRACTICE OF EJACULATORY PRAYER

We are convinced that the majority of souls who crave for holiness would ask for nothing better than to be often thinking of God. But how is this possible?

In the first place, we can train ourselves to think of God *from time to time*. The easiest method, to begin with, is to make an act every time that there occurs some marked change of occupation. " If we can," writes St Teresa, " let us practise many times a day the exercise

of the presence of God, or at least now and
then. . . . The recollection of the Com-
panion within us, were it to last only but
a moment, would be of an immense profit
to us."

Fénelon enters into more details : " Profit
by the moments in the day when your mind is
only partially occupied with external things
to think of God interiorly ; for example, do
your needlework in the simple and familiar
presence of God. It is only while we are
talking that recollection is less easy : neverthe-
less we can often recall to our minds a general
thought of God which will act as a check on
our words, and will repress the susceptibilities
of self-love in our dealings with our fellow-
creatures. We should be careful not to take
too large a share in all that is said and done,
and not to let these things fill our minds.
Once we have seen what God demands of us
in each instance, that is sufficient, and we can
stand apart from all that follows. In this
way the centre of the soul will remain free
and tranquil. . . . An excellent method of
keeping ourselves in this interior solitude and
freedom of spirit is at the finish of each act
to bring all our reflections to a full stop, and to
give up all after-thoughts whether of joy or
sorrow, for these are some of the greatest
hindrances. Happy the mind that dwells
only upon what is of importance, and only
thinks about each act when it is the right

moment to do so." Then, after some further excellent advice, he concludes with these words: " Let us separate ourselves from all pleasures that do not come from God, and restrain useless thoughts and day-dreams and the repetition of idle words." There is another passage from his works which deserves mention: " A brief recollection of the presence of God during meals, especially when they last a long time and there are many pauses, will serve to keep you within the limits of sobriety and to fortify you against excessive daintiness. There are moments at table when conversation lags because the guests are busy assuaging their appetites; this is an opportunity to give a thought to God; but all this should only be done so long as the thought and the wish for it come naturally into the mind without being forced." [1]

These last words of Fénelon, " so long as . . . without being forced," should be remembered. The great law which governs the spiritual life, taken as a whole, is to avoid carefully all that can hinder " the holy liberty of the children of God "—that is to say, everything that curbs it, and prevents its free spontaneous action, and disturbs the mind so that it loses its peace and serenity.

We have read in the lives of some of the Fathers of the desert, and in the biographies of certain saintly persons of our own time, how

---

[1] Fénelon, *Instruction and Advice*, vol. i, p. 530.

they reached the most alarming figures in the number of their ejaculatory prayers.[1] It is recorded of St Leonard of Port Maurice, for example, that he made the resolution to repeat the invocation: "My Jesus, mercy," a thousand times a day, either mentally or vocally. It was revealed to St Mary Magdalen of Pazzi that St Aloysius made unceasing aspirations which, to use an archaic expression, were shot like arrows from a bow up to heaven; and she herself made the offering of the Precious Blood fifty times a day for the souls in purgatory. St Francis Xavier repeated so frequently the words "O most Holy Trinity!" that the heathen learned the habit of saying it also, although they had no idea what it meant. Father William Doyle, the well-known Irish chaplain in the late war, wrote in his diary six months before his death: "I have a clear inspiration that God asks me to make a hundred thousand ejaculations in a day. I feel that our Lord asks this in reparation for his priests."

---

[1] In the well-known *Vitae Patrum*, it is related of a saintly recluse that he raised his heart to God a hundred and three times during one conversation; and it is noteworthy that the hermits and early monks were unused to making long prayers. St Augustine, in a letter to Proba, writes: "It is said of our brothers in Egypt that they prayed frequently, but that their prayers were very short, like darts shot heavenwards, and the reason for this is interesting: it was for fear that the attention would end in becoming dulled and be extinguished finally if the prayer were prolonged."

Is it necessary, in order to reach divine union, to seek to emulate these privileged souls and to aspire to these heights, or at least to force ourselves to make these stupefying mathematical calculations ? Not at all.

If it is good in principle that our ejaculatory prayers should be as numerous as possible, and that the interval between them should be as short as can be, it is also important that the rhythm of their frequency should be subject to the following two rules laid down by spiritual writers, Alvarez de Paz in particular, because he always tries to establish the exact equilibrium between the exertions prompted by generosity, and the need of the soul for rest. The first is to guard against the weariness that speedily leads to distaste, and secondly, to follow the leading of grace, for the Holy Spirit does not demand the same measure from all. It may be noted that a certain type of distaste comes not from over-exertion, but from pure laziness, and therefore is not a lawful motive for abandoning our good practices. But directly our conscience, aided if necessary by the advice of our director, tells us before God that we ought to bring them to an end, then it is our duty to do so. The habit of monthly recollection and the annual retreat, above all, have in part the object of adjusting these difficulties in our spiritual life.

Whatever happens we should never be surprised, and, above all, on no account be dis-

couraged if in spite of our good resolutions—
and it is only these circumstances to which
we are referring—we do not at the outset
attain to the allotted number of ejaculations,
or if we discover that they are fewer to-day
than yesterday. Man is well known to be an
inconstant being, and while on this earth he
is much less likely to march on from one
victory to another than to be perpetually
retracing his steps.

Father Caussade, in his book *L'Abandon à
la Providence*,[1] dwells upon this fact: " No
one should be surprised that a day when
recollection is easy is followed by another
crowded with distractions, for such is our
condition in this present life. These variations are necessary even in spiritual matters,
so as to keep us in a state of humiliation and
of dependence upon God. The saints themselves went through these alternations."

All this is very edifying, some persons will
say, but our difficulty lies neither in the
initial generous impulse nor in the wise
manner of putting it into practice. We ask
for nothing better than to think about God.
But *how can we remember to think about him?*
When we are carried away by feelings which
get the upper hand and dominate us, how
can we manage to free ourselves at certain
moments and pierce through to the supernatural even if only in a lightning flash?

[1] Vol. ii, letter xvii.

We have seen how the practice of daily meditation (to pray carefully) and the exercise of the virtue of continual detachment (turning everything into prayer)—that is, an elevation to God by a pure intention and not a descent to self by following some whim of the moment—will facilitate our contacts with the invisible world. But it may happen, even after a carefully prepared meditation and a scrupulous effort at detachment, that the soul is so engrossed by external affairs and a victim of circumstances that she will find great difficulty in recollecting the explicit presence of God. She may pass several hours, a complete morning, or the whole day without a single thought of her divine Guest or making one ejaculatory prayer. She wanted to remember him, but she forgot to do so. What can be done?

As the world of sense is the great obstacle, the best method is to try and connect a pious thought with some ordinary act, thus turning an enemy into an ally. To utilize some detail of our everyday life to remind us of the spiritual world. St Ignatius, as an experienced psychologist, is careful to base his scheme of particular examen upon this characteristic of human nature, for he advises us to combine the spiritual considerations with an exterior attitude or gesture.

For example, it is agreed upon that every time we pass some sacred figure, or a crucifix, or even when performing some commonplace action such as leaving the house or going into a room, or similar acts, they will remind us of the presence of God. Peasants used to make a knot in their handkerchiefs so that they might not forget some detail. Father Maunoir, after his missions in Brittany, asked his congregation to sew a heart-shaped piece of stuff on their sleeves, red for the men, and blue for the women, so that in the middle of their work in the fields or the home the sight of this coloured patch might recall to their minds the thought of God. The repetition of the Angelus serves the same pious purpose.

Is there any danger that this frequent withdrawal into the interior life may be detrimental to the duties of our state of life ? Not at all, if common sense is used. On the contrary, as St Francis de Sales is careful to remark, it cannot fail to put more heart into our work, and to make us more conscientious and generous-minded in our work. "Note clearly," he writes, "that the practice of ejaculatory prayer is neither difficult nor incompatible with your occupations, and far from diverting or lessening your attention to your business, it will render it easier and more efficacious."

It is evident, all the same, that the more manual the type of work the less risk of it being in any way interfered with by the explicit exercise of the presence of God.

The more intellectual the occupation we are engaged upon, the more it absorbs all our thoughts, and only by making a violent effort is it possible from time to time to break off and interpose a thought or say a word about God. In such a case we should be misunderstanding our duties if we were to attempt such a thing. If ejaculatory prayer hinders our work, then it must be sacrificed, so that the work may be properly done; before all things, the duties of our state, as has been said already. St Ignatius Loyola, when he was a university student at Paris, felt himself suddenly overpowered by the realization of God's presence during the lectures. Acts of divine love came bursting forth from his heart, and followed one another without interruption. He seemed to be in heaven. That is true, but he was not attending to the class. He quickly realized that his studies were bound to suffer from these holy transports, so he asked God to repress them in order that he might be able conscientiously to complete his studies. Here is an intelligent form of piety.

But which are the best ejaculatory prayers? Are there some that should be preferred to others?

The answer to this question is that each person should choose what he prefers; this is the main point. At one time his inclinations will lead him to follow some inspiration from his prayers, or from the words of the liturgy, or perhaps it may be rather the cry of the soul who is in the purgative way : "*My Jesu, mercy; have pity on me !*" On another occasion the aspirations will turn towards the illuminative way : "*Jesus, be to me a Jesus !*" which was the favourite invocation of St Philip Neri ; or the popular ejaculation : "*Sacred Heart of Jesus, I have confidence in thee !*" Other persons may choose the ejaculations suggested by the unitive way, that are the best of all and which more readily minister to its needs : such as, "*O Blessed Trinity !*" the exclamation of St Ignatius, or "*My God and my all !*" of St Francis of Assisi, and many others.[1]

Without denying the utility of these suggestions, it may be added that in the case of a soul that has no special learnings or attractions, it might use the *Sign of the Cross* or the *Glory be to the Father* as ejaculatory prayers of the highest value. It is good in general that our spiritual life should have its own fund to draw upon and not be encumbered by foreign vegetation. Before adopting pious practices and methods, let us first utilize what we have already tried. How many times in the day do we make the *Sign of the Cross*, and the *Gloria*, especially if we have an office to say. The *Gloria* was the favourite ejaculation of St Jerome. He sent it to Pope Damasus, who decided to add it to the breviary at the end of each psalm. It is impossible for the

---

[1] See also Rodriguez, *Christian Perfection*, vol. i., chap. iii.

priest to think of the words in each verse as he repeats his office, but what an easy and helpful way it is to try and recollect himself, or rather to recollect the Holy Trinity in each *Gloria !*

What better reminder of the presence of God !

At this point it will be useful to draw attention to the enormous advantage gained by those persons who have chosen, not the presence of God in all around us, but his presence *in us*, as the centre of their spiritual life.

The search for God present outside demands a certain effort of the imagination, which results in a greater struggle and subsequent fatigue. The return to God present within us presupposes a simple glance of faith. The divine indwelling in a soul in a state of grace is a reality which requires no composition of place, nor that, in order to reach it, I should set off on a sort of audacious and fantastic pilgrimage to the confines of space ; I have only to enter into my interior, and God is there. Father Brou remarks that " Of all the methods of trying to enter into the presence of God, this one (to find God within the soul) is perhaps the most efficacious— at least for those who have the habit of prayer —and is the one which the saints most recommend." [1]

[1] *St Ignatius, Master of Prayer*, edition Spes, p. 54.

The words *In the name of the Father* do not cause me to think of the Father millions of miles away, or who dominates me with his immensity so that my heart is more frightened than softened, but of a Father close by and within me. In the *Name of the Father* who is there, and, to use an expression of Father Faber's, who finds a *home* in me of the Son, who is waiting for me at the door of my heart, and the Holy Spirit who intervenes in the conduct of my life so to impart to it its eternal merit, who does everything with me and will not leave me for one instant alone.

We have seen how the thought of God present in our souls through grace is the great dogmatic truth on which a life of recollection can be most easily founded.

Everyone who has become familiar with this thought has an admirable method of practising union with God, whether alone or in company, and of utilizing his surroundings as a means of leading him back to his centre.

When we are alone with ourselves, a double self accompanies us always. If we have sufficiently developed the spirit of faith; if we realize the gift of God and truly believe, and if for us the words "God is within us" are not only a beautiful phrase, a fine theme for a pious dissertation, but an undeniable fact that exists; if the expression "We are the living tabernacles of Christ and in very truth his holy temples " has the value of reality for us —can it be impracticable or difficult to be recollected on all occasions ?

When we go into a cathedral or church, instinctively the voice is lowered, we walk quietly. The great God is present, the divine Host : let us be silent and adore.

Whatever we have to do, whether it be our business, some household shopping, a recreation, a course of study, so long as it is our duty, it will be quite impossible to get away from him who is living and dwelling within us.

We are a living cathedral. Each one of us is his own chapel. And provided we are in a state of grace, God lives and dwells within us. What then ?

The conclusion to be drawn is very simple and easily reached. It is that we must live and act as if we were dwelling in a church in the presence of the Tabernacle.

The Holy Eucharist is not the only sacrament of the Real Presence ; there are two, Baptism and the Holy Eucharist. The presence of the three Persons of the Holy Trinity in us through Baptism is no less real than the presence of our Lord in the Tabernacle ; the difference lies in the mode of their presence, not in the reality. How comes it, then, that when we leave the church we behave as if the Real Presence had ceased ?

It is because we have not sufficient faith, and that in practice we do not know the gift of God.

Our spirit of recollection outside the church should be as profound as it is within the church. The monk, a disciple of St Bernard, who composed the *Meditationes piissimae*, wrote: "Wherever thou art, be recollected. There is no need for a special place. Thou art thyself this special place. Art thou in bed? then thy bed is itself a temple."

The sole difference will be due to the duties of our position here and there.

I go into church to join in some service or to say some private prayers. But when I go out, I carry with me my tabernacle, I bear within me the Real Presence; therefore all I have to do will be done in the company of the divine Guest, with the *dulcis hospes animae*. I shall not become immobile in static adoration, because my duties oblige me to work. But I shall not work in a turmoil, without an aspiration of adoring love, for my faith reminds me of the Guest whom I bear within me, that I am a living ciborium.

I am busy, because it is my duty. But I do not work without God, because the most high God never leaves me alone.

Can we imagine a more luminous doctrine, at any rate in principle, or one simpler or more stimulating and apt to incite the soul to make unceasing cries of appeal, a loving gesture, a sign that will testify to him who is always present that we are not absent, but fully recognize the imcomparable value of his continual presence.

" Faith tells us," writes St Paul of the Cross, "that our heart is a large sanctuary, because it is the temple of God, the dwelling-place of the Holy Trinity. Often visit this sanctuary, see that the lamps are alight—that is to say, faith, hope, and charity. Frequently stir up your faith when you are studying, working, or feeding, when you go to bed and when you rise and make aspirations to God."

In a seventeenth-century book, entitled *Practices for Keeping in the Presence of God*, we are recommended to give " a simple but loving thought to God present within us." By *simple* is implied that it can be done without pictures, acts, or mental reasoning and effort of the brain : nor does this manner of thinking of God get into the way of occupations, it assists them ; it is easier to work in the presence of a friend. By *loving* is meant that this exercise is always accompanied by a secret longing to please God as a sign of our love for him present in us, but it is not necessary to make a particular act of the love of God.

St Teresa is the great authority on this matter, it is to her we should listen, and we need not hesitate to give a long quotation from that fine chapter xxx of the *Way of Perfection*.

" St Augustine tells us that after searching for a long time to find God in the things that surrounded him, he discovered him at last within himself. Meditate deeply these words, for it is of great profit for anyone that has difficulty in recollecting himself to understand this truth : to know that it is not necessary for him to raise himself to heaven in order to converse with his divine Father and find his happiness with him, nor to elevate his voice so as to be heard ; God is so near that he hears the slightest whisper from our lips and the most secret thought. We have no need of wings to go in search of him : let us enter into the solitude and look within us, it is there that he is. Let us talk with him in great humility, but also with love, like children talking with their father, confidently telling him our troubles and begging him to help us, and recognizing above all that we are not worthy to bear the name of his children."

Then, in order to reassure those persons who will be astonished to see her pushing her practices to such far-reaching consequences, she adds these words : " Those who are able to recollect themselves in the manner that I have just described, should know that they are walking on an excellent road and they will not delay in drinking of the fountain of life."

There follows an injunction to under-estimate no longer the gift of God, as is so often done.

" If men were careful to remind themselves that they possess a guest of such majesty, it would become impossible for them to devote themselves with such blind enthusiasm to the things of this world, for they would see how worthless they are beside those that they possess." She ends with this following valuable advice :

" For myself, I own that I never knew what it was to pray with satisfaction until he him-self vouchsafed to teach me this salutary method. Let him who desires to acquire this habit of the presence of God, never weary of working little by little to gain the mastery over himself, by recalling his senses within himself. Far from losing, he will find therein a great gain for his soul, that of retrenching the exterior use of the senses and of making them subservient to his interior recollection. If he speaks, let him try to remember to address One in the depth of his heart ; if he listens, let him not forget that he must listen interiorly to him who speaks within. In short, let him consider that if he will, he can always enjoy this divine company. Let him practise this many times a day, if possible ; if not, let him at least practise it sometimes. Provided that in the end he becomes accustomed to it, he will sooner or later derive great benefit from it. When once this divine Master has given him this grace, he would not exchange it for all the treasures of the world. In the name of God, since nothing can be gained without labour, do not grudge the time and application that you have given to it. I assure you that with the help of our Lord, you will succeed in one year, or perhaps six months."

A last word remains to be said on this important matter. Even in the world in our customary and necessary contact with others, our household duties, our works of charity and of apostolic zeal, our society and business relations, the full realization of the gift of God will be of greater assistance than anything else in keeping the recollection of the presence of God.

God is living in us. But he lives also in the neighbours who are moving around us. Here also he is living or wishes to live; therefore, knowing that we are surrounded by tabernacles either actual or by destiny, what an easy reminder they become of the three divine Persons.

Nor is there here any effort of the imagination, or laborious composition of place, which some persons declare to be beyond them. It is sufficient to consider that which is a reality. There is no need to construct, simply to make a statement, not to create, only to realize the value of this truth.

Let us imagine the case of a young mother busy with the multiple cares of her children. She must not say, " Union with God is impossible for me." She is surrounded with tabernacles of the Real Presence. Her little ones are baptized? Yes! Then God is living in them.

This master, this factory hand, foreman, worker, school child, our colleagues, and those we employ—are they not, if not in fact, at any rate potentially and by destiny, the bearers of Christ? Why look for anything else in them? Or at least why should we not see in them also, and above all, this one dominant fact? The " gift of God " is not meant only for us. It is also for them. They were created and placed in the world for a divine destiny. Our Lord shed his precious blood for them. Their earthly work is nothing else but their means of reaching heaven and of enjoying by grace the anticipated possession of the three Persons of the Holy Trinity, while awaiting the fullness of glory.

A deeper understanding of this doctrine will undoubtedly help us to remember these facts.

II

THE ADVANTAGES OF EJACULATORY PRAYER

It is natural that ejaculatory prayer and the exercise of the presence of God should be recommended by the teachings and personal experiences of the great spiritual writers and saints. One or two extracts of a specially striking character are added to those that have been given already.

" We should look for the presence of God in all things," writes St Ignatius Loyola, " in our conversations, our walks, when we are using our eyes, listening, or thinking, when we are eating, and in all that we do. This manner of meditating, which causes us to find God in everything, is easier than the method which obliges us to exert ourselves, to elevate the mind to the consideration of more abstract truths. This salutary practice, if we dispose ourselves rightly, will be rewarded by a gracious visit from our Lord, even if it lasts only for the duration of a short prayer. Let us accustom ourselves to offer our troubles and difficulties frequently to God, and remind ourselves that we accept them out of love for him, sacrificing our own wishes to be of service in some way to his divine Majesty, by aiding those for whom he accepted death that they might live. We should examine ourselves upon these two points."[1]

"The shortest road to attain to divine charity," says Louis of Granada, "is to raise our hearts to God by our strong affections and by desires that are on fire for his love by conversing with him with respectful confidence, and keeping ourselves always recollected in his presence."[2]

St Francis de Sales and St Leonard of Port Maurice give the same advice. St Francis de Sales writes: "The essence of real devotion lies in this exercise of spiritual retreat (recollection) and in ejaculatory prayer. It can supply the lack of other prayers, but if it is missing, nothing can take its place. Without it, it is impossible to follow the contemplative life properly, and the active life will be a failure." He continues, speaking of this "retreat of the heart," with the words: "It is here, Philothea, that I wish you to be most docile in following my advice: for it is upon this that your spiritual progress is most dependent."[3] And during the retreat preparatory to his consecration, the great Bishop made this resolution: "I will do my best to make ejaculatory prayers during the day."

[1] St Ignatius, *Epistles*, pp. 223-226.
[2] Louis of Granada, *The Love of God*, chap. ix, p. 126.
[3] *The Devout Life*, chap. xiii.

G

The celebrated Italian missioner, St Leonard of Port Maurice, echoes the same idea. " Would you like to have your paradise anticipated upon earth ? and the company of someone who will lead you rapidly to perfection? . . . Live in interior recollection and walk in the presence of God." Then, speaking of himself, he says : " My vocation is mission work and solitude. My mission is to be always working for God. All the rest is nothing." And each one of us has a like vocation did we but realize it.

The saints and spiritual writers are so unanimous and impressive in their recommendations, that there must needs be wonderful advantages to be gained by the habit of ejaculations and the practice of the presence of God.

And this is quite true.

The first of these advantages is that prayer and detachment become easier, and as we have seen, they are the two fundamental methods of attaining to union with God.

To render prayer less difficult we are told : " It is quite certain that when we love something the thought of it comes often into our minds, but it is true, also, that this frequent thinking about it will greatly increase our love. One who is faithful in recollecting the presence of God frequently, will soon be all on fire with love, and in proportion as his love increases, so his thoughts of him will become so continuous that he will not forget him any more." [1]

Not only does prayer like this become easier by the exercise of the presence of God, but also throughout the day the life of interior silence, so necessary for union with God, will be facilitated. A solitude in which we perceive only the emptiness of life is not very attractive ; but if we have the skill to people it with thoughts of the supernatural, then this solitude appears to be no longer dark and sad, but rich and splendidly dowered, and overflowing with life, and how alluring! Those only who cultivate the presence of God, and the habit of frequently raising their hearts to him, can know, as Cardinal Manning expressed it, " that solitude and silence are full of reality."

In the same way, the use of ejaculatory prayers facilitates detachment. We are usually so craven-hearted because we do not realize clearly for whom and for what reason we ought to gain the mastery over self : the thought of God, particularly when it is inspired by ardent love, acts upon the dying embers of our life like a breath of wind, which blows away the dust that has accumulated, and awakens the spark, kindling it into flame.

These words do not exhaust all the advantages of the use of the exercise of the

[1] D'Argentan, *Le Ciel dans l'âme chrétienne*, p. 23.

presence of God and of ejaculatory prayer. There is much more to be said. There is no better method of developing a *state* of continuous moral union with God, than the frequent repetition of these acts of union. The term moral union is used because, as was said at the beginning of these pages, a continuous actual union is impossible save by a special grace of infused recollection, owing to our very limited powers of attention.

At the commencement, there should be a reasonable effort to think of God for a certain number of times, and to offer him our different actions. Then, little by little, will come an ever-increasing desire to do more.

There should be nothing feverish or hurried, but an harmonious, virile, and loving development, of the spirit of faith, so that supernatural habits having become natural, we turn back to the centre of all, dwelling within us, whenever nothing external demands our attention, to the service of the King. As soon as I am obliged no longer to work for God, then I will think about him; this is the rhythm of the practice of a recollection that aims at being both prudent and intense.

Thus we shall possess, or are preparing ourselves to possess, a continuous union with God; the habit of raising ourselves to God has become such a part of our lives, that it may be called uninterrupted. It is not a case of saying words, but the heart remains clinging to

God, the will is one with the will of God, and
the volatile mind, that is so often distracted
and not always through its own fault, is so
attentive to purify or offer its intentions before,
during, and after the occupations of each
moment of the day, that, in truth, to borrow
the comparison of St Francis de Sales, the soul
resembles a child who is picking flowers by
the roadside, but never lets go of his father's
hand. St Thomas calls this a habit, a stable
quality that assists us to act without difficulty.
It is characteristic of a habit that it is something that comes easily, and the habit of
prayer, in common with every other habit, is
the fruit of perseverance.

A modern philosopher gives a good descrip-
tion of the gradual self-mastery that is always
progressing until at last the habit of union
with God becomes quite easy. " The first step
in interior progress consists in the development of certain psychological states. At first
the mental powers are turned in upon themselves, and having but rarely the opportunity
of outward expression, they seem to acquire
an importance which they do not possess as
yet. . . . The faithful Christian, whose love for
God at first consists in a brief recollection
night and morning, reaches the point of being
able to perceive the continuous presence of
the object of his love with him, even when a
voluntary effort seems to be required to enable
him to fix his attention upon vocal prayer;
he feels himself from henceforward to be

obsessed by the need of praying. . . . Soon
he begins to look upon the universe as merely
a transparent veil, behind which the presence of
the Creator can be everywhere discovered. . . .
Every creature, however humble, is an image
of the face of God. Thus he recognizes in all
the mark of God, revealing their common
origin, so that in his eyes they will appear as
all brothers and sisters of each other and of
him. In this way, out of his first effort
to turn himself towards God, has grown up,
like the tree from the acorn, a devouring love
of God and of all things in God."[1]

Then we have the lyric language of Father
Gratry :

" There are persons that feel more than
others the need of rest and of the return to
the centre of life. When such a one has
united himself to God, has tasted of his fullness,
after having been subject to the insufferable
vanity of the outer life, there comes a time
when all business, all external work, all going
into the world, becomes impossible to him.
The world is then like an intruder who comes
to disturb a feast, and the necessity of sub-
mitting to it draws tears ; as when some
tedious business comes upon us in the midst
of an inspired work, or some stranger, one
we know by sight, but whom our heart
knows not, comes in and takes up the best

[1] *Essai sur la Vie Intérieure*, by E. Gilson, in the
Revue Philosophique, January-February, 1920, p. 31.

part of the day that had been promised to prayer and study, and by his words, countless and unprofitable as the dust, distracts our attention, which fails at every word to concentrate itself. Even thus does the outward life weary these persons and increase their longings for the eternal rest. It is true that such a ripeness for death is rare among men; but the least can comprehend and accept it." [1]

If we are among these " least," we ought not to be too surprised that we have still to struggle in order to attain to the desired habit of recollection, and we should have confidence.

But how comes it that in spite of a normal power of attaining good habits and the assistance of grace that trebles our own powers, yet we do not reach our goal?

St Teresa avows that "For years I was going through the trial of being unable to fix my thoughts . . . it was extremely painful. But I knew that our Lord condescends to keep us company when we go to him humbly to ask him for it. If a year passes without our getting there, very well then! let it be several years. I assure you that we can reach it, and we can with effort acquire the habit of living thus in the company of the greatest of all masters." [2]

[1] *Meditations,* by Father Gratry, pp. 106-7.
[2] *Way of Perfection,* chap. xxvi.

On his side Louis of Granada says: "The holy King David tells us that he lived always in the presence of God, when he uses the words: 'I set the Lord always in my sight.'[1] Do the same thing, and raise your heart continually to God, without violently forcing yourself, but letting your mind lose itself in loving simplicity in this sovereign Divinity. Do not be distressed to find your thoughts so often distracted owing to human weakness: try quickly to recollect yourself and offer yourself to God anew. If you have the courage to go through this combat without being shaken for some length of time, I venture to assure you that the custom will become second nature, and that not only you will no longer have any difficulty in recollection, but even that you will never give it up. You will be like the fish that cannot live out of water, and if it finds itself outside, does all that it can to return."[2]

The soul that easily and habitually turns towards God in the midst of its ordinary occupations, possesses a moral union that is continuous.

If at this moment it should please God to call us to a state not of acquired recollection, but to that which is infused, nothing will have done more to prepare us for this favour—as far as it is possible for us to prepare for what

[1] Ps. xv 8.
[2] Louis of Granada, *Amour de Dieu*, chap. ix, p. 130.

is a pure gift of God—than the effort to remain in the presence of God as continually as is humanly possible, through the exercise of the spirit of faith and of loving generosity.

St Teresa, whose advice upon this point is based on her own personal experiences, declares that " In this way you are laying down a solid foundation. And if it please our Lord to raise you to higher things, he will find you ready." [1] St Teresa was here referring principally to the habit of recollecting the presence of God within us.

This is not the place to seek to penetrate into the realm of "higher things" to which the saint alludes. To do so would be to go beyond the scope of this book, which is to show how, with the aid of grace such as is common to us all, *and the co-operation of our own personal resources*, it is possible to reach union with God, and to arrive at that degree of recollection which is obtainable through our own spontaneous efforts.

For those others to whom God vouchsafes the gift of infused recollection, whether by a touch or a prolonged state, they no longer require counsels and rules, but should practise the virtues of docility and humility and make the donation of their whole selves without reserve.

[1] *Way of Perfection*, chap. **xxix**.

The Holy Spirit himself takes over their guidance, and he leads them without the sound of words.

The writer of this volume may also be silent, and utilize the silence as it ought to be used at the termination of a work, in asking our Lord to bless those who will read these pages and to give to them the largest possible share in the joys of " praying always."

CONCLUSION

IF this little book were to have only one reader, and that reader unknown to us but so greatly beloved in Christ Jesus, we should not wish to end it otherwise than with these words of advice. They come from the lips of a master of the spiritual life, perhaps the greatest of all masters, St John of the Cross. "Why have you been putting off for such a long time your going to God, since *at this very instant* you can occupy your heart with loving him?"

If, on the other hand, he is one who has already resolved to belong to God, and his whole heart is occupied at this moment with loving him, but he would like to love him more, a passage from the same *Spiritual Sentences* of the saint will go far in reassuring him. "If you desire a clear and simple view of God in your soul, and that he should there shed his radiancy, do not busy yourself among creatures; on the contrary, empty yourself of them, then you will walk in the midst of the divine light."